Date Due

BRODART, INC.   Cat. No. 23 233   Printed in U.S.A.

Canada | The Land That Shapes Us

PHOTOGRAPHY BY MALAK

KEY PORTER BOOKS

Canadian Cataloguing in
Publication Data

Malak
Canada | The Land That Shapes Us
ISBN 1-55013-667-4

1. Canada - Pictorial works.
I. Newman, Peter C., 1929–
II. Title.

FC59.M35 1995   971'.0022'2
C95-931211-0   F1017.M35
1995

Key Porter Books Limited
70 The Esplanade
Toronto, Ontario
Canada M5E 1R2

95 96 97 98 99 6 5 4 3 2 1

Pages 2–3: At Peggy's Cove, Nova Scotia, an angry sea lashes the rocky coast. *1977*

Pages 4–5: The skyline of Montréal, Québec, at dusk, with Mount Royal, an extinct volcano, in the background. Montréal has the distinction of being the world's second-largest French-speaking city, and a major inland seaport. *1992*

Pages 6–7: Waterton Lakes National Park, Alberta. Established in 1895, this park covers 52,000 hectares (200 square miles) and is linked with Glacier National Park in Montana. *1977*

Pages 8–9: The wheat fields of Saskatchewan – a sweeping vista of sun-washed crops that underlines the important role of the prairie provinces in the Canadian economy. *1978*

Pages 10–11: Pisew Falls on the Grass River, Manitoba. *1978*

Pages 12–13: Mount Orford, in the Appalachian Mountains of Québec, is renowned as a cultural and ski centre. *1992*

Page 15: Ottawa's Peace Tower seen through a tracery of snow-laden boughs. *1949*

Page 17: Dutch tulips surround the National War Memorial in Ottawa, honouring the memory of Canadian soldiers who gave their lives to liberate the Netherlands during the

Second World War. *1951*

Page 19: Fundy fishermen were Canada's Lobster Kings. His face etched by sea, wind and sun, this lobster fisherman from Wedgeport, Nova Scotia had a gross income of $3,000 a year from lobster fishing, but only $800 was clear profit. Live lobsters were first shipped from Nova Scotia to Boston in 1872. *1942*

Page 21: A Gatineau log driver carrying his peavey is living proof of many encounters with logs. *1948*

Page 26: Malak by wife, Barbara. *1995*

Page 27: My favourite model – my daughter, Marianne Karsh – started posing with tulips at the tender age of three months. Here, at nine months, she happily shows her early love of tulips – a love shared by her father. Photographs of Marianne appeared in thousands of newspapers and magazines, and on posters. The Dutch Bulb Growers named a pink daffodil and a red amaryllis for her. *1962*

Page 50: The Flowerpot Rocks at Hopewell Cape, New Brunswick. The Bay of Fundy's giant tides eroded and shaped the red cliffs into these strange, fascinating formations. *1977*

Page 51: Fortress Louisbourg, Nova Scotia. *1970*

Page 82: The business and downtown area of Toronto – the capital of the Province of Ontario – photographed at dusk from the CN tower. *1993*

Page 83: Autumn maple leaves. *1994*

Page 122: A rainbow, the traditional symbol of hope, arches over a landscape near Calgary, Alberta. *1987*

Page 123: Whistler Convention Centre with Mount Whistler, British Columbia, in the background. *1994*

Page 146: Fishermen slip cautiously past an iceberg the size of a twelve-story apartment building, in Cumberland Sound, Baffin Island, Northwest Territories. Only one-ninth of the iceberg is visible above the waterline. *1982*

Page 147: One of the best ways to fish for arctic char on Baffin Island, Northwest Territories, is by hiring local Inuit guides, who are expert in directing anglers to the most likely areas. The arctic char, a member of the salmon family, is prized as both a sporting game fish and a flavourful meal. *1982*

Page 160: This lumberjack displayed a "fantastic hand" during a break in work during the spring log drive. *1948*

To my brother Yousuf, who made it possible

for me to come to Canada,

and

to my wife and lifetime collaborator

Barbara

and our children, Sidney, Michael,

Laurence, and Marianne

CONTENTS

PREFACE

YOUSUF KARSH

When my brother Malak came to Canada in 1937, it was the fulfilment of his dream, and the beginning of his lifelong love affair with his new country. To breathe the air of freedom, after a boyhood of oppression, was exhilarating. Malak joined me in my studio and quickly developed into a fine photographer, his desire to explore Canada melding with his technical expertise.

We both were fascinated with portraits: I with the ever-changing features of the human face, and Malak with the many-faceted landscapes — the face of Canada and its people. For over half a century, Malak's insatiable curiosity and restless wanderings have taken him over the length and breadth of this country, to record its essence. The earliest photograph in this book dates from 1940; the most recent was probably taken just before this book went to press.

Whether recording the joy of ice-skating on the Rideau Canal, Canada Day fireworks on Parliament Hill, the hushed, sepulchral beauty of an iceberg in the Northwest Territories, the myriad reflections of autumn leaves of Ste Adèle, Québec, aglow in the half-light of dusk, or the lonely poignancy of an endless road amid the wheatfields of Saskatchewan, Malak brings to his work his unerring eye and unconditional love — and patient endurance! Sometimes, to capture the moment, one must wait an eternity — until the light is perfect, until the shadow is graphic, until the rain has stopped, or until the view from the small, lurching airplane spirals towards the decisive image.

If Canada is partly defined by its landscape, Malak has shown us, over the years, the beauty, the diversity, the soul of our country. I am proud to write the introduction to a retrospective celebration by a superb photographer who happens to be my brother.

THE LAND THAT SHAPES US

PETER C. NEWMAN

C anada's least disputable characteristic is size, and my favourite illustration of just how considerable a hunk of geography we occupy is the argument used a few years ago by Private Justin Dwyer, stationed with the 2nd Canadian Infantry Brigade near Soest in West Germany, objecting to a transfer to a Canadian army camp at Jericho Beach in British Columbia. He lodged an official complaint, pointing out that the move meant he would be 5,627 kilometres away from his family home at Grand Falls, Newfoundland, 804 kilometres farther than this NATO service in Germany.

That small example shows vividly the size of this country, and it is our outrageous dimensions that give shape and reason to our identity as Canadians. A West German ambassador in Ottawa once concluded, "I have a country; you have a continent." He was right. Canada laid over a map of Europe would reach from the west coast of Ireland and stretch deep into Asia, east of the Ural Mountains into the heart of the Soviet Union. Ottawa would be located roughly at Kiev, the capital of the Ukraine. It takes six time zones to accommodate Canada's vast expanse, so that when it's 4:30 in the afternoon in Newfoundland, clocks are chiming high noon across the Yukon.

Canada also happens to be the world's most awkwardly designed country. The unwieldy dispersal of our population decides the nature of Canadian life; it affects everything we do in that we have to deal with small numbers of people over enormous distances. The ratio of transportation costs to eventual market price is complex enough to deal with in terms of commodities, but it is very much more difficult for transmitting ideas, culture and emotions from east to west, from north to even more north, and back again. There is so much more to geography than space. Marshall McLuhan was correct when he postulated Canadians' unique relationship with nature: "We go outside to be alone, and we go inside to be with people – a pattern that is antithetic not only to Europeans, but to all other cultures."

That link to the outdoors is reflected not only in our psyches but in our looks. Canadian historian William Kilbourn once observed, "Outnumbered by the trees and unable to lick them, a lot of Canadians look as though they joined them – having gone all faceless or a bit pulp-and-papery, and mournful as the evening jackpine round the edges of the voice, as if something long lost and dear were being endlessly regretted." When Dale Benson, location manager for the movie sequel *Rocky IV*, was asked why he chose to shoot it in Vancouver, his down-to-earth reply was that he had picked British Columbians to portray rugged Soviet citizens watching Sylvester Stallone beating their hero to a pulp because "Californians look too pretty. You people look like you've really lived."

It is the streak of nordicity in our national character that makes us look that way. Territorial integrity (holding on to our turf, that is) remains our strongest sustaining myth. We happily give away our energy resources and minerals at rock-bottom prices, and we sell to foreign investors the most profitable parts of our secondary manufacturing sector. But let a Yank demand one drop of our water or sail through the Northwest Passage, and we respond with outrage. That's why arctic sovereignty, fishing rights and acid rain (or, for that matter, Québec separatism, which was perceived by most English Canadians as a threat to the physical continuity of our reach from sea to sea) have become such hot issues.

It sometimes seems that despite our 128 years of history as a nation, we are barely a country at all. Yet we have performed miracles to get as far as we have. To carve even that sliver out of the wilderness which we now occupy has been an epic of Homeric proportions, a silent battle against the cold and the wind and the rocks. Canada is larger than China, with a population smaller than Ethiopia's. Yet less than seven percent of Canada's landscape is actually settled, and something like three-quarters of Canada's population is squeezed into less than one percent of the country's land area – nearly all of it hugging the United States border. Of our 125 cities, 102 are within 300 kilometres of the American boundary. Most of our hinterland broods silent and inaccessible, an empty land filled with wonders.

Because of such population concentrations, there is a curious skew in the way Canada is perceived by both strangers and native sons. Since exploration and development unyieldingly followed an east-west progression, the centre of the country is usually thought to be located around Winnipeg. In fact, Canada's exact middle is at Baker Lake, an old Hudson's Bay Company trading post at the head of Chesterfield Inlet, off Hudson Bay.

Apart from our elephantine geography, a favourite rationalization for Canadians' sense of identity is our climate: six months of winter followed by six months of bad sledding. It really does get cold – even in our large cities. Regina has recorded temperatures of –50°C, and temperate Vancouver once hit –20.

Only the Mongolian capital city of Ulaanbaatar is colder as a capital than Ottawa.

The land's moods, seasons and weathers are the chronometers by which we measure our lives. There is nothing benign about the Canadian landscape, and the epic of civilizing its contours was mostly about hard lives and the anguish of pioneering families discovering themselves and each other too little and too late. Yet it is the land that anchors our sense of who we really are.

"There would be nothing distinctive in Canadian culture at all," says the greatest of our literary critics, Northrop Frye, "if there were not some feeling for the immense searching distance, with the lines of communication extended to the absolute limit, which is a primary geographical fact about Canada and has no real counterpart elsewhere. Everywhere we turn in Canadian literature and painting, we are haunted by the natural world, and even the most sophisticated Canadian artists can hardly keep something very primitive and archaic out of their imaginations."

Given that mystical relationship to the land, it remains one of the great ironies of Canadian topography that an astonishing 37 percent of our Class One agricultural land (on which you can grow almost anything) lies within sight of the top of Toronto's CN Tower – and that so little of that rich loam is still being cultivated or ever can be again.

Perhaps our most powerful geographic feature is the St. Lawrence River, every inch of it, in Hugh MacLennan's magnificent phrase, "measured and brooded over by notaries and blessed by priests." It provides the great Canadian metaphor, defining the emotional difference between arriving on our shores and arriving on the American eastern seaboard, where you step from the wharf directly into the social and commercial heart of that country. "One enters Canada," Northrop Frye has written, "through the Strait of Belle Isle into the Gulf of St. Lawrence, where five Canadian provinces surround us, with enormous islands and glimpses of a mysterious mainland in the distance, but in the foreground only sea and sky. Then we go up the waterway of the St. Lawrence, which in itself is only the end of a chain of rivers and lakes that starts in the Rockies.... To enter the United States is a matter of crossing an ocean; to enter Canada is a matter of being silently swallowed by an alien continent."

That 1,200-kilometre journey up the St. Lawrence, so quickly and blithely bypassed by the airlines, ought to be a requirement of Canadian citizenship. It was from the quays along this shoreline that the voyageurs set off along the rippling, rugged rivers that cleave the hinterland. They were in the service of the fur trade, the commerce that first gave substance to the notion of Canada as a transcontinental state. They crossed the Prairies and later the Rockies, claimed the watersheds of the Mississippi and Columbia and fanned up into the subarctic. They rode the great Churchill River, which roared down to Hudson Bay from the divide at Lac La Loche, site of the infamous Methye Portage, the longest and toughest on the trade routes. Conquering its 20-kilometre trail by climbing a 180-metre elevation under 40-kilogram packs of freight and furs earned voyageurs the ultimate badge of courage. After crossing this formidable rampart, the canoes were in Athabasca Country, whose gloomy forests eventually yielded the world's most prodigious fur catch.

The impact of these transcontinental trading routes was pervasive enough to work the magic that helped save Western Canada from being absorbed into the United States. Holding the land claimed through right of exploration, and later by occupation of the Hudson's Bay and North West companies, was a close call, but it was the scattering of those puny fur-trading outposts that held the line.

One of the essential differences between the geographies of Canada and the United States is that American rivers, such as the Mississippi and Missouri, run across populated basins, giving focus and direction to the communities of their shores. With such exceptions as the St. Lawrence and the Fraser, most of our major rivers run northward, unwatched and unknown. Few Canadians have ever seen, or will ever see, the country's longest river, the mighty Mackenzie, whose drainage basin ranks next in size only to the Amazon and the Mississippi.

Our image of ourselves is based largely on the contours and colours of our North. It was into our mysterious attic that the Group of Seven painters journeyed most frequently to find their subjects and inspiration. Inventing new techniques to capture the breathtaking magnitude of what they saw, they broke with European schools of painting to refine their exploding vision and put it to canvas. "We came to know that it is only through the deep and vital experience of its total environment that a people identifies itself with its land and gradually a deep and satisfying awareness develops," Lawren Harris reminisced after one northern journey. "We were convinced that no virile people could remain subservient to, and dependent upon, the creations in art of other peoples.... To us there was also the strange brooding sense of nature fostering a new race and a new age." In the pages that follow, Malak Karsh of Ottawa has provided his own evocative image of the country – its shimmering colours, its shifting moods, and the real reason why this vast land shapes us.

While no single factor forms a nation's character, winter's dominance and the North that symbolizes it, rank among Canada's most potent influences. "I've always felt that in Canadians' novels the geography, nature, is not a background, it's a character, as it is in Russia," Canadian novelist John Ralston Saul once explained. "Canadian fiction is much more like Russian fiction than it is like American or English or French."

To most Canadians, North is less a place than a direction – the ultimate reflection of how we view ourselves in relation to the land we call home. "When we face south," contends novelist Margaret Atwood, "our conscious mind may be directed towards crowds, bright lights, some Hollywood version of fame and fortune – but the North is at the back of our minds, always. There's something, not someone, looking over our shoulders; there's a chill at the nape of the neck. The North focuses our anxieties. Turning to face north, we enter our own unconscious. Always, in retrospect, the journey north has the quality of dreams."

Most city dwellers, especially in Central Canada, seldom travel any farther northward than their summer cottages. Yet we are all marked by the wild. As historian W. L. Morton pointed out, "Because of our origin in the northern frontier, Canadian life to this day is marked by a northern quality. The line which marks the frontier from the farmstead, the wilderness from the baseland, the hinterland from the metropolis, runs through every Canadian psyche."

Morton was right. Even in contemporary and highly urbanized Canada, our landscape is our lifeblood. Being Canadian means paying heed to the country's seasonal rhythms, turning our inner ear to the land's music. "From the land," decreed historian A. R. M. Lower, "must come the soul of Canada."

INTRODUCTION

MALAK

W hen people ask me if I would choose photography as a career if I had to make that choice again, my answer is emphatically yes. I know no other profession that would give me the same sense of fulfilment. Every picture I am about to take represents a new and different challenge, never boring, always exciting. This becomes exhilaration and joy when I succeed, utter despair when I fail. The feeling is both emotional and personal. My work is really an endless journey of discovery, even when I am working in a familiar environment. I may have photographed the same subject many times, but I always look for something new. For example, I have photographed the Parliament buildings in Ottawa many times, but always I try to discover new dramatic possibilities and interpret them — images that may be created by unusual light conditions, such as clouds or fog.

Practising this way of life and work requires both personal dedication and the support of one's family. Fortunately, right at the beginning of my career I found the ideal partner and wife. Since our marriage in 1942, Barbara has tolerated my unusually long hours of work and frequent absences on assignment and travel. She has done this in spite of the heavy burden of running the business and raising our four children, Sydney, Michael, Laurence, and Marianne, of whom we are very proud. Barbara's artistic talents and sound advice have been indispensable to me throughout my career.

I was born in 1915 in Mardin, Armenia, in Turkey, a small picturesque town of stone houses and orchards of fruit trees. Here we tasted manna, a very sweet substance which falls like dew on the leaves of trees. It is thought that this was the same food that sustained the Israelites during their exodus from Egypt in biblical times. When I was a very small child, towards the end of the First World War, our family emigrated to Aleppo, Syria. Father, Mother, Yousuf, Jamil and I travelled on foot with one donkey loaded with our few possessions. For my father, travelling in this manner was a normal way of life. In earlier years he had driven caravans of donkeys and camels from Mardin to Iraq as he pursued his export/import trade.

Our family consisted of Father, Mother and four sons. Mother was a scholar and read the Bible daily. Father could neither read nor write, but, he had an exceptional memory and a computer-like mind that could recall details of all his commercial transactions with his clients. For his children he had one abiding goal, and that was to provide them with an opportunity to acquire the best possible education. For our very poor family that was a tall order. The eldest son, Yousuf, attended a Franciscan school, while my brothers Jamil and Salim and I attended an American missionary school, where we studied courses in Arabic, English and French. I graduated from high school with honours. Only Jamil, with the financial help of Yousuf, was fortunate to attend the American University of Beruit and graduate in medicine. To this day, all four of us gratefully acknowledge our father's fanatic belief in the advantages of education, regardless of the sacrifice this might involve.

I arrived in Canada in 1937, at the suggestion of my brother Yousuf and with his help; he was already well known for his portrait photography. Yousuf and I are the third generation of our family to come to this country. It began with our great-uncle Aziz Setlakwe, who came to Canada in 1904, the first Armenian to settle here. Arriving penniless, he settled in Thetford Mines and made a living by peddling dry goods, on his back, to farmers and rural communities in the Eastern Townships of Québec. Years later, he established the first department store in Thetford Mines, flying his own distinctive pennant. Over the years he financially assisted a host of relatives and friends to come and settle in this wonderful country. Among those who benefited from his generosity was our uncle George Nakash, a prominent photographer with a studio in Sherbrooke, Québec. Uncle Nakash in turn helped Yousuf to emigrate, and subsequently provided him with training in photography. Our great-uncle Setlakwe's great-grandchildren live in Thetford Mines and other areas of Québec, and still play important roles in their communities.

My first day in Canada remains vividly etched in my memory. It was October. Yousuf had taken me hiking in the Gatineau Hills, north of Ottawa, where the trees seemed on fire with brilliant autumn foliage. I had never imagined that such glorious colours were possible. That first impression had a profound influence in shaping my future life.

For the ensuing three years I apprenticed with Yousuf, learning the fundamentals of photography in the darkroom. There I had the opportunity to observe Yousuf's mastery of lighting, composition and the art of portraiture. I was also able to watch his critique of photographs shown at Camera Club meetings, and this was a wonderful way to learn.

This, my most published photograph, was taken in 1963. Pulpwood logs floating on the Ottawa River were directed by tugboats to the E.B. Eddy Forest Products Mill in Hull. The picture was reproduced on the back of the one-dollar bill in 1974, and, following the continuous issue of 3.5 billion notes, remained in use until the dollar bill was replaced by the Loonie in 1987. *1963*

In 1939 I was getting anxious to start taking my own pictures. During a walk on Wellington Street in Ottawa I noticed the old Sacred Heart Church in Hull, its graceful spire glimpsed through a hole in the wall of an old building that was being demolished. Not owning a camera, I hastily borrowed one from a friend passing by, snapped the photograph and submitted it to the United States picture magazine *Coronet*. It was titled "Out of the Ruins," and to my surprise and unforgettable joy it was accepted and reproduced on a full page. I was rewarded with my first cheque. It looked better than a million dollars. I felt that a gate to the world had opened for me, that I must walk through and take my chances in a competitive milieu.

In 1941, with my brother's enthusiastic support, I decided to open my own studio, specializing in commercial photography and pictorial journalism. To avoid capitalizing on Yousuf's reputation, I chose to use my first name, Malak, for my business. I rented space in an old building on Sparks Street and immediately advertised for a secretary. A young lady, Barbara Holmes, born in Saskatchewan, who was just finishing business college, responded to my ad, attracted by the words "artistic secretary." I hired her, and in no time she was printing my black and white photographs, typing all copy and generally running the studio while I went on out-of-town assignments for the *Star Weekly*, *Saturday Night* and the *Montreal Standard*. It was an auspicious beginning: Barbara later became Mrs. Malak.

During the early years of the war I covered a variety of interesting assignments, including a flight to Newfoundland in a B-24 bomber, sitting on an orange crate, to photograph the Atlantic Coastal Command, Canadian and American troops in Newfoundland, and sailors' lives in a submarine and on the escort ship *Quinte* in mid-Atlantic.

At that time I had to deal with problems arising from the use of my first name. In Halifax, the Military Police detained me at least ten times due to confusion caused by my credentials. Both the RCMP and military HQ had identified me simply as Malak, while my passport showed me as Malak Karsh. The security guards were naturally suspicious of allowing a person loaded with cameras into a most sensitive military area. In the end, all went well.

In January 1943 I was asked to photograph White River, Ontario, reputed to be the coldest spot in Canada. The night I arrived the temperature was minus 49.4°F. As I stepped off the train my first breath felt like swallowing razor blades. The next day it was minus 54°F. I was worried that my cameras might cease to function in such cold weather, but as the air was so dry that problem did not arise. There were some interesting effects, as when steam rising from the trains seemed to freeze and hang in the air in a long low white stream. The men who maintained the railway operations wore at least five suits of underwear to survive the cold, but one brave young lady posed for me in a bathing suit and bare feet for a few seconds. She survived, but had to thaw out in the hot bath awaiting her.

Shortly after the White River assignment, I caught a severe cold. It developed into tuberculosis and I had to spend three years in the Royal Ottawa Sanatorium. When I left the "san" my doctor warned me against working for myself and suggested I seek employment with regular hours. I applied to a department store and was offered a salary of thirty-five dollars a week; this I declined. A few days later, I took a picture of the Peace Tower framed by snow-laden trees and submitted it to the advertising department of the same store. They loved it, and published it on a full page carrying their New Year's message for 1946. The amount they paid for that one-time use was one hundred and fifteen dollars.

In 1953 Donald Cameron, director of the Banff School of Fine Arts, invited me to give the first course in photography offered by the school. Knowing the magnificent location of Banff, I found the invitation irresistible. On arrival, I discovered that I had thirty students with varying photographic skills. In our first session I told them that I was not going to be a "lecturing teacher." Instead, we would learn while we took pictures. I divided the students into two groups, juniors and seniors — according to their levels of experience, not their ages. Thus a lady of seventy found herself in the junior class, while a teenager was in the senior group. My students had plenty of models from other classes to photograph against the magnificent mountains, waterfalls and wildlife. However, this sometimes backfired. When we invited the music class to perform in the nearby forest for the resident elk population, some of the latter became so irritated by the sound of the violins that they charged. We had no casualties, but we got the hint and ran for dear life.

At this point in my career, I began to develop an extensive library of scenic and pictorial images, an invaluable source for submissions to newspapers and magazines. I discovered that managers in industry were keen to use photographs telling the story of their industrial achievements to the public. I was soon offered the opportunity to photograph some of Canada's major industries, such as plants producing pulp and paper, textiles and aluminum. The resulting pictures, accompanied by informative articles and with appropriate captions, were submitted to daily and weekly newspapers and to magazines. The acceptance rate quite astonished me, and the features were published in large numbers.

When I was photographing the Aluminum Company of Canada operations in Kitimat, British Columbia, I forgot myself in the enthusiasm of seeing a different angle and stepped backwards onto the crust of a tank of molten aluminum, which fortunately was thick enough to bear my weight. An inch less of crust and I would have become part of an aluminum ingot.

On another occasion, while I was photographing the spring log drive near a dam, I asked two lumberjacks to hold my stepladder on some closely packed logs to enable me to get a better view. As the logs were being pushed downriver the stepladder gave way, and I was plunged into the icy water. It was all I could do to hold my cameras over my head while I was being rescued.

When I am working, I need to concentrate all my attention on the various elements that constitute the picture. I tend to ignore anything likely to distract me from the task at hand. Sometimes this has resulted in embarrassment, as on the occasion when I was photographing the new building of the Canadian Museum of Civilization in Hull. While I was on top of a high stepladder, a gentleman tapped on it below. Desperate to meet a deadline, I motioned him away, saying that it was impossible for me to speak to him then. I later learned that I had chased away Douglas Cardinal, the architect of the building I was photographing — a man I had been very anxious to meet.

I had a frightening experience while photographing the RCMP Musical Ride in Rockcliffe. I particularly wanted to record the thrilling last moment of "The Charge," when men and horses come thundering to the final stop. I had previously noticed that the area where they usually trained often became dusty, obscuring the action, and at my suggestion the Superintendent moved the riders to a grassy field.

I stationed myself within a few feet of the finishing line and the Mounties charged. But the horses were unfamiliar with the new field, and would have trampled me to death had it not been for the superhuman efforts of the riders, who managed to stop them just a few feet from me. I got the picture, though, and it was great.

Logging operations of the pulp and paper industry offered picturesque possibilities from the photographer's point of view. Before the opening of roads in the Gatineau, north of Ottawa, I travelled by train, horse-drawn carts or sleighs, according to season, to photograph lumberjacks at work. I spent Christmas with them and their families in order to produce the story "Christmas in the Bush," published widely in 1949. For years photographs of Mounties and logging operations were the images of Canada most favoured by foreign publications, and the photographs I took were reproduced hundreds of times in Canada, the United States and other countries. Logging pictures were frequent winners in Canadian photographic competitions, and at the fifth annual Salon of Commercial and Press Photography, organized by the Professional Photographers of Canada, I was the only competitor awarded three firsts. The jolly, barrel-chested lumber-camp chef, his arms loaded with crusty loaves of freshly baked bread, won first prize in the illustrative class and was judged the best commercial photograph in the show. Another winner was a picture of a logjam being dynamited. To get this I had to be in a safe place designated by the foreman of the log drive. Anxious not to miss the shot, I arranged for an assistant, a lumberjack, to take another picture from a different angle with instructions to click the shutter when he heard the explosion. I was lucky to get my picture, but my assistant didn't have the same faith in his fellow lumberjacks. At the sound of the blast he threw my camera, a new Graflex, into the river and ran for his life. The camera was never recovered.

One of my pulp and paper pictures – the most widely published – had the unique distinction of being selected for printing on the one-dollar bill. This photograph, taken in 1963 to illustrate paper and politics, showed thousands of pulpwood logs floating on the Ottawa River below Parliament Hill. The dollar bill went into circulation in 1973 and was withdrawn by the Bank of Canada in 1987, to be replaced by the Loonie.

While my photographs of industries were popular with the media, in the 1950s I developed another use for them. We prepared sets of twenty photographs, each illustrating an industry, and sent them to boards of education in the various provinces. Printed to a 16x20 inch size with fifty-word captions, mounted on hardboard and coated with plastic spray to preserve them while in transit and during use, these photos were shown in city schools of most provinces. Photo sets on the Canadian Broadcasting Corporation, the nylon industry, aluminum manufacturing, the pulp and paper industry, immigrants, the making of power cable by Northern Electric and other subjects were shown in classrooms. With educational authorities beginning to recognize the value of visual aids, this presentation was found to be very useful. Besides showing students the fascinating inside stories of Canadian industries, they were helpful for classes in geography, art, layout and design, literature, history, essay-writing, public speaking, as well as vocational guidance – an interesting extension of my career objectives.

In the spring of 1946, I photographed the first tulips ever grown on Parliament Hill. Little did I know then that taking pictures of tulips would become a dominant part of my career lasting forty years.

Those first tulips were the thank-you gift of Princess (later Queen) Juliana of the Netherlands for Canada's hospitality to the Dutch royal family during the Second World War. The photographs I took of tulips with the Peace Tower and National War Memorial were published extensively in Canada and many other countries. After seeing my photographs, the Associated Bulb Growers of Holland appointed me their official photographer and Canadian representative.

My assignment was to show the home gardener the beauty of spring flowers and gardens through my pictures and accompanying informative copy. Canada's ideal climate for growing spring-flowering bulbs helped me to convey this message to gardeners. To get photographs to illustrate beautiful gardens I travelled frequently to Holland, across Canada, particularly British Columbia, and on occasion to the United States and England.

I always needed models, and I happened to have one handy at home: our baby daughter, Marianne. From the age of three months to ten years when she decided enough was enough of "Just one more, please," she posed with daffodils, crocuses, hyacinths and tulips, and appeared in countless publications and on award-winning posters. Consequently there is now a handsome daffodil called the Marianne Karsh, and a scarlet amaryllis as well. The best her father could do was a tulip named the Malak Karsh, a red/mauve triumph tulip registered in 1984.

Queen Juliana's gift of tulips to Ottawa and hundreds of thousands of Dutch tulips, daffodils and crocuses purchased by the Federal Government helped the National Capital Commission gardeners create the most spectacular flower beds of any city in the world. Every spring, I happily took a new crop of pictures, which were published widely in newspapers and magazines.

In 1951 I suggested the idea of establishing an annual Canadian Tulip Festival to the Ottawa Board of Trade, which they immediately adopted. To their lasting credit, board members volunteered countless hours of their time to realize this. The festival got underway in 1953 and became an immediate success attracting many thousands of visitors from Canada and the United States. Canadian prime ministers William Lyon Mackenzie King, Louis St. Laurent and John Diefenbaker all posed on bended knee to do their part in ceremonial bulb plantings in the fall.

The success of the Canadian Tulip Festival had far-reaching influence on the cultural and recreational life of Ottawa as it encouraged the establishment of a string of festivals throughout the summer and winter months, including Winterlude in February, which features skating on the Rideau Canal, the world's longest skating rink.

Although I have photographed almost every part of Canada, it is Ottawa, the national capital and my home town, that has claimed the greatest part of my time. It continues to challenge me.

Recent additions to the city's architectural diversity have attracted worldwide interest. The National Gallery of Canada, designed by Moshe Safdie – a treasure of granite and glass rising like a giant candelabrum on the banks of the Ottawa River, within close proximity to the Parliament Buildings – houses the national art collection. The Canadian Museum of Civilization, an unusual design by Douglas Cardinal, links Canada's past with its future in two buildings, The Canadian Shield and The Glaciers. Photographs I have taken of these buildings have appeared in most of the world's leading architectural magazines, and my collection of pictures of the Canadian Museum of Civilization has been published in a book bearing the same title.

During my travels across Canada I have found myself mesmerized by the overwhelming beauty of the land, no matter where I happen to be. Whether on the promenade of the Château Frontenac in Québec City, watching the ships on the St. Lawrence River, standing on the shores of Nova Scotia or the red soil of Prince Edward Island, visiting the fishing coves of Newfoundland or watching the icebergs drift past Baffin Island, gazing at the haunting beauty of Lake Superior's rugged coastline, the magic of the Prairies, the majestic Rockies and mountains of the west coast, I have always felt proud to be able to say, "All this is my country, and I am both fortunate and grateful to be a part of it."

The career I chose back in 1941 has fulfilled my ambitions and my dreams far beyond any hopes I could have entertained at the time. I have had the chance to portray the magnificence of Canada, and something of the indomitable spirit of the people of all races who are fortunate enough to inhabit it.

These are the feelings which have led me to enter with dedication and enthusiasm into the preparation of this pictorial portrayal of Canada, my adopted and beloved country. The selection of a representative portfolio of my work of the past fifty-five years has brought back to Barbara, my wife and colleague, and to me, precious memories of past experiences of trials, tribulations and gratifying successes. We hope the portfolio will engender unforgettable memories in all who examine it.

Right: "Out of the Ruins" – my first published picture. It shows the Sacred Heart Church (later destroyed by fire) in Hull, Québec, seen through a gap in the ruins of Ottawa's old Supreme Court building. *1939*

Below: White River, Ontario – Canada's coldest spot. It was minus 48°C (minus 54°F) when this picture was taken. Steam rising from the train froze almost instantly, and hung low in the windless atmosphere. *1943*

Left: A picture of wife Barbara, with sons Sidney and Michael (taken for the dairy industry), capturing the mood of the morning milk delivery – now a memory from the past. *1949*

Below: This group photo was taken at the Well Baby Clinic of the Victorian Order of Nurses. It was widely published to illustrate a newly introduced cotton diaper and, later, the postwar baby boom. *1948*

Above: Winter, with its cold, snow, ice, skating, skiing, and tobogganing, can be a time of sheer happiness for children, as well as a traditional part of Canadian life. *1940*

Right: Children watching the Long Sault rapids near Cornwall, Ontario. These rapids disappeared when the waterway became part of the St. Lawrence Seaway. *1951*

During the Second World War many farm wives took
over the work on the land, including such heavy tasks
as ploughing. This picture was taken in western
Québec. *1940*

A Canadian rite of spring – a log drive on the Tomasine River, north of Maniwaki, Québec – an activity which has contributed immeasurably to the early life and economic development of Canada. *1948*

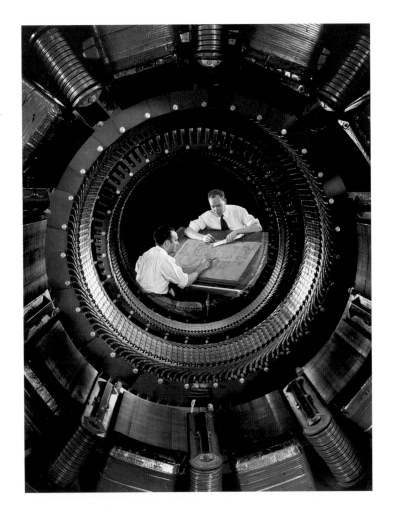

Left: This photomontage shows "stators" used in hydroelectric plants, and the electrical engineers who designed them at the Canadian Electric plant in Peterborough, Ontario. *1951*

Below: Polymer Corporation, Sarnia, Ontario, was founded in 1942 to produce synthetic rubber, because of the acute wartime shortage of natural rubber. Here, Polysar butyl rubber is extruded before being milled into sheet form. This synthetic rubber remains the basic material for the manufacture of such modern essentials as airtight inner tubes. *1952*

The staff of life – wheat being unloaded at
Québec City, Québec. *1956*

At dawn: Miners reported for the early
morning shift at an underground mine in
New Brunswick. *1959*

Aluminum, the most abundant of the metals used by man, requires large amounts of inexpensive electric power to separate the metal from its ores – power easily supplied by Canada's vast hydroelectric resources. These Alcan Tri-Lok ingots are specially designed to fit together and were en route to the markets of the world from the smelter at Kitimat, British Columbia. *1959*

An airport on the Mid-Canada Line, a radar warning system, at Great Whale on Hudson Bay, Québec. After every snowfall the airport's runway had to be cleared – a herculean task calling for a huge snowplough that tossed a spume of snow high into the air. *1959*

Left: A display of woollen fabrics photographed for the textile industry at Renfrew Woollen Mills, Renfrew, Ontario. *1948*

Below: Sheep proudly show off their lambs to visitors at the Central Experimental Farm in Ottawa, Ontario. This photograph was taken for the textile industry. *1952*

In 1953 I taught the first course of photography offered at the Banff School of Fine Arts. Both students and I had wonderful opportunities to photograph students in other classes. One of our favourites was the ballet class directed by Gweneth Lloyd, assisted by Eva Von Genesy. Here, ballerina Eva Von Genesy "flies high" over the Rockies. *1953*

PART ONE

THE EAST

An aerial view of the coast of Prince Edward Island. *1987*

Above: The lighthouse at Tryon Head. The red soil of Prince Edward Island adds drama to this beautiful seascape. *1987*

Following pages: The lighthouse of Baddeck, Nova Scotia, at dawn. Baddeck is renowned as the home of Alexander Graham Bell, inventor of the telephone and early researcher in human deafness and aeronautics. *1987*

Icebergs drift south from Greenland past Bonavista,
Newfoundland, one of the oldest communities in
North America. *1991*

The city of St. John's, Newfoundland. Well-maintained houses cling to the hills behind the waterfront, a mosaic of colour against an otherwise drab landscape. Reminiscent of old cities in Europe, St. John's is unique in Canada, and a source of inspiration to photographers. *1963*

The world's longest covered bridge at Hartland,
New Brunswick, 391 metres (1,282 feet), was built
in 1899 over the Saint John River. *1977*

The Angus L. MacDonald Bridge. This impressive
441-metre (1,447-foot) bridge spans Halifax harbour,
Nova Scotia, a busy port in peacetime and a major
staging-post in both world wars. This is one of the
longest suspension bridges in the British
Commonwealth. *1987*

Salvage Cove, in eastern Newfoundland. This small
fishing village is the oldest continually inhabited
community in the province. *1990*

Signal Hill, at the entrance to St. John's harbour, Newfoundland, was once an impregnable fortress guarding the city. The hill was named for its signal cannon in the sixteenth century, but in 1901 Guglielmo Marconi took up a strategic point on the hill to receive the first transatlantic radio message, inaugurating a new era in international communication. *1983*

Left: The *Bluenose II* under sail in Halifax harbour, Nova Scotia. This is a 1960s replica of Canada's most famous ship, a boat that doubled as a fishing boat and racing schooner that was almost undefeated in the 1920s and 1930s. *1990*

Above: Fishing for bluefin tuna off the coast of Prince Edward Island. The world record for tuna caught by rod was set here in 1978, with a fish of 560 kilos (1,232 pounds). *1972*

Redfish, delicious to eat and one of the family of
flatfish. They are marketed in stores as "ocean perch."
Newfoundland. *1976*

Above: Peggy's Cove, a favourite destination for photographers and artists as well as tourists, is famous for its lighthouse and rugged coastline and for the image it presents of a typical Nova Scotia fishing village. *1987*

Following pages: Long Point Lighthouse, near Twillingate, Newfoundland, was built in 1876. From the tower there is a commanding view of the Atlantic, with brilliant sunsets, and ice floes from the Labrador Sea. *1992*

Their boats locked in the grip of winter's ice, fishermen at Port de Grave, Newfoundland, await the
spring thaw. *1973*

Neil Harbour, Cape Breton, Nova Scotia. Lobster
traps and fishing boats are evidence of an industry
that has provided generations of Nova Scotia inshore
fishermen with a way of life, while supplying
gourmet fare for seafood lovers in both Canada and
the United States. *1987*

An apple orchard near Cape Blomidon. Huge
quantities of apples are grown in the Annapolis
Valley, one of Nova Scotia's most fertile farming
areas. *1992*

A charming stretch of pastoral coastline near
Charlottetown, Prince Edward Island. *1959*

The Spanish *conquistadores* found potatoes in the Andes
and took them home to Europe; years later they were
brought back to the New World, and they now
flourish in Prince Edward Island. *1976*

Above: Acadian Historic Village at Caraquet, New Brunswick. Staff wearing traditional costumes harvest flax which is carded and spun to produce linen, re-creating one feature of Acadian life between 1780 and 1880. *1977*

Following pages: Farmland and valleys around the Minas Basin in Nova Scotia can be viewed and enjoyed from the Cape Blomidon Lookoff. This region was home to the Micmac Indians. *1979*

Atlantic salmon attempt to scale Big Falls on
Newfoundland's Humber River, in Squires Memorial
Provincial Park. Though most Atlantic salmon weigh
four to five kilos (nine to eleven pounds), specimens
five times that size have been recorded. *1983*

Fishing on the Miramichi River, New Brunswick, famous for salmon. Anglers from many countries try their luck here. *1992*

Beaver love carrots. In a pond in Barnesville, east of
Saint John, New Brunswick, Mr. John Mickelburg
taught them to obey the command "Come on up";
the beaver would waddle in close to gently grasp
the food. *1979*

L'Anse aux Meadows, Newfoundland, a United Nations World Heritage Site, is the first known Norse settlement in North America; it dates back to about 1000 A.D. The national park features a re-created sod village with living quarters and workshops. *1983*

The Sandstone formations at Cavendish are a striking
feature of Prince Edward Island National Park. Thin
layers of sand and mud were deposited by ancient
rivers two hundred million years ago. Under the
pressure of their own weight, the layers hardened into
sandstone and mudstone that were later eroded by ice
and water. *1982*

The long stretches of sandy beach at Cavendish,
Prince Edward Island, attract tourists in large
numbers during the summer. Cavendish was the
home of Lucy Maud Montgomery, whose world-
famous story *Anne of Green Gables* helps draw countless
visitors from around the world to this location. *1976*

PART TWO

CENTRAL CANADA

Meech Creek, Dunlop Park, in the Gatineau Park,
Québec, a short drive from Ottawa. In winter this
area becomes a skiing centre for cross-country and
downhill enthusiasts. *1991*

When the land sleeps. . . . Trees in winter garb. *1994*

Previous pages: Early autumn morning mist crowns golden hills of Algonquin Park, Ontario. *1990*

Above: Sunrise on Parliament Hill, Ottawa, Ontario. Canada's national Capital. *1966*

A glorious winter day – minus 40°C (minus 40°F) – at
Whitney, Ontario. *1987*

Flowerpot Island is named for this pillar of eroded limestone, 17 metres (55 feet) high. It is near Tobermory, in Georgian Bay, Ontario, and is part of Fathom Five – Canada's first underwater national park. *1974*

The Scarborough Bluffs, just east of Toronto, rising 60
metres (200 feet) above Lake Ontario, are among the
most unusual geological formations in North America.
The layers of clay and sand provide a record of the last
ice age. *1991*

Above: A red trillium in Cantley, Québec. Most of the trilliums in this region are white, but a few are of the less common red variety. *1987*

Left: Canada geese in flight at Jack Miner's bird sanctuary at Kingsville on Lake Erie, Ontario. *1969*

Fishing at dawn on the Ottawa River near Pembroke,
Ontario. *1974*

Above: At Dunrobin, Ontario, a traditional "snake fence" covered with ice assumes a magical look in the light of the setting sun. *1969*

Following pages: Jacques Cartier Park, 40 kilometres (25 miles) north of Québec City, Québec. High rising hills and winding rivers with whitewater stretches are found in an area of just a few miles. Sunlight shining through a cloudy sky becomes a giant spotlight, creating mystical images. *1992*

Right: A Kwakiutl-style raven transformation mask by
Beau Dick in the Grand Hall of the Canadian Museum
of Civilization in Hull, Québec. *1994*

– 98 –

Above: Modern sculpture "La foule illuminée" by
Raymond Mason in front of the National Bank of
Paris/Laurentian Bank Towers on McGill College
Avenue, in Montréal, Québec. *1992*

Previous pages: A tapestry of colourful Dutch tulips in
Major's Hill Park sets off this view of the Parliament
Buildings, Ottawa. Over two million tulips bloom in
time for the Canadian Tulip Festival in May of each
year, a glorious start to spring. *1992*

Above: Sainte-Adèle, the jewel of the Laurentians,
Québec. The attractive homes are built on the slopes
of Mont Sainte-Adèle, around Lac Rond. *1983*

Above: Saint-Siméon, with its modern church, on the south shore of the Gaspé Peninsula, Québec. *1990*

Following pages: Hot-air balloons fly over the Ottawa River during the Gatineau Hot Air Balloon festival in Québec. *1994*

Cranberry harvesting at the Johnstone Cranberry
Marsh, Bala, Ontario. *1985*

A farm near Foldens, in southern Ontario. *1987*

The last log drive on Baskatong Reservoir in the northern part of the Gatineau, Québec. Harvesting of the forest in this region began in 1806. Logs were floated downriver to mills in Hull and Ottawa to be processed into lumber, pulp or paper. After 1991, no more logs were sent down the Gatineau River – the end of an historic and picturesque transportation mode. *1991*

Above: Maple sap being boiled down into syrup in the old traditional way at Upper Canada Village, Morrisburg, Ontario. *1988*

Following pages: Saint-Benoît-du-Lac – a Benedictine abbey with an Old World look on the shore of Lake Memphrémagog, Québec. *1976*

Above: A farm in Cantley, Québec. *1963*

Right: Farmers from the Mennonite community near Kitchener, Ontario, go to Meeting in horse-drawn buggies. *1977*

Above: Fireworks display "crown" over the National Gallery of Canada in Ottawa, Ontario. *1995*

Left: The famous RCMP Musical Ride executes "The Charge," a dramatic finale to an exciting performance. *1972*

The Aberdeen Pavilion, built in 1898 in Ottawa, Ontario, as the centrepiece of the Central Canada Exhibition, is a rare 19th century large scale exhibition building. (It was designated as a National Historic Site in 1983.) Known to local residents as "The Cattle Castle," it housed agricultural shows for many years. Recently renovated, it now accommodates trade shows, sporting events and a variety of social functions. *1994*

Mont Tremblant Provincial Park, Québec, located 140 kilometres (88 miles) from Montréal, has hundreds of lakes, three large rivers, waterfalls and countless streams. Winter turns the park into a fairyland of snow-draped trees, and a playground for alpine and cross-country skiing, snowshoeing, and snowmobiling. *1984*

This ice sculpture in front of the National Gallery of Canada, Ottawa, called *In Your Hand*, represents the "Peace on Earth" theme. It was carved during Winterlude by Venezuelan artists Max Zulete and Reynolds Pache to commemorate the 50th year of the mandate of the United Nations. *1995*

The statue of Lt.-Colonel John By, builder of the
Rideau Canal and founder of Ottawa, stands high on
the cliff rising from the Ottawa River and facing the
Parliament Buildings, Ottawa, Ontario. *1994*

These students are members of the Canada Sea-to-Sea Expedition, organized to commemorate the 200th anniversary of Alexander Mackenzie's crossing of the North American continent by travelling in heavy canoes, wearing eighteenth-century costumes. On their way up the Ottawa River they stopped to visit the Canadian Museum of Civilization in Hull, Québec. *1993*

Under a canopy of frost-laden trees, skaters glide on
the world's longest skating rink – the Rideau Canal –
during Winterlude in Ottawa, Ontario. *1993*

PART THREE

THE WEST

Previous pages: The moon rises over a mountain near Whistler, British Columbia, one of Canada's most popular ski resort areas. *1994*

Above: Manitoba grows over 90 percent of Canada's sunflowers. While some seeds are sold as snacks, most are processed into sunflower oil, margarine, mayonnaise, and animal feed. *1974*

Tofino, on the western shore of Vancouver Island
near Clayoquot Sound, British Columbia. Disputes
over logging practices in this magnificently scenic area
have aroused international public concern. *1993*

When the crops are ready for harvesting in the
Province of Saskatchewan – world famous for its
wheat – grain farmers race against time to take
advantage of good weather. *1966*

Swathed ripe grain, formed into intriguing patterns,
is left to dry completely before it is combined.
Saskatchewan. *1978*

The overwhelming beauty of the afternoon sun
shining on Maligne Lake, Alberta – framed by majestic
mountains – makes pleasure fishing a mystic
experience. *1981*

Little Qualicum Falls, on Vancouver Island, flows
from a lake high on a mountain in British Columbia.
1981

Left: Fishing below the Nistowiak Falls, northern Saskatchewan, on the Churchill River. *1993*

Above: Golden rails in the setting sun symbolize the challenge which shaped the character and culture of the early pioneers who settled in the Canadian Midwest. *1976*

The romantic, fertile Qu'Appelle Valley,
Saskatchewan. *1993*

Above: A cattle roundup in Turner Valley, Alberta. Taken during a snowstorm, this photo captures the eternal struggle between man and the elements. *1972*

Following pages: Vancouver, British Columbia, at dusk. One of Canada's beautiful cities sparkles like diamonds at night. *1987*

The British Columbia Legislature, in Victoria. *1993*

Northwest Coast Indian artifacts on display at the
Museum of Anthropology, University of British
Columbia, Vancouver. In the foreground is a
Kwakiutl feast dish carved from a cedar log. *1993*

It took years to develop wheat strains to suit Alberta's
frigid winters and short growing season, but wheat is
now one of the country's primary crops. *1981*

Above: Cowboy at the Calgary Stampede, Alberta, one of the premier rodeo shows of North America. *1977*

Following pages: Sunrise over the Sasagiu Rapids on the Grass River, Manitoba. *1978*

Buffalo roam freely in Manitoba's Riding Mountain
National Park. *1977*

The old Prince of Wales Hotel overlooks Waterton-
Glacier International Peace Park, Alberta. *1977*

PART FOUR

THE TERRITORIES

Purple fireweed, the official floral emblem of the
Yukon, waves in beauty beneath a summer sky.
Fireweed spreads rapidly after forest fires, hence
its name. *1961*

The Arctic is like a frigid desert, and the flowers that blossom as if by magic in its short summer seem all the more colourful against the stark landscape of rock, sand, and snow. This large-flowered wintergreen is at Igaliut (formerly known as Frobisher Bay), Northwest Territories (now known as Nunavik). *1982*

The late spring breakup on the Yukon River near
Whitehorse, forerunner of the short Yukon summer.
1982

Horses grazing near Whitehorse, capital of the Yukon
Territory. *1982*

Right: Pangnirtung Fiord cuts 45 kilometres (28 miles) into Baffin Island, Northwest Territories. On both sides of this narrow chasm, sheer rock walls plunge abruptly into the sea. This beautiful region is the starting point for many adventurous expeditions. *1982*

Above: The ice breaks up in Pangnirtung Fiord, Baffin Island, Northwest Territories. Both visitors and local Inuit eagerly await this time so they can go fishing and camping. *1984*

Above: The White Pass and Yukon Railway which, at one time, was an important transportation link between Whitehorse (the capital of Yukon Territory) to Tidewater at Skagway, Alaska. The rugged but awesome beauty of the country traversed masks the hardships of the intrepid men from throughout the world who flocked to the Klondike Gold Rush of 1898 via "difficult to climb" Chilkoot Pass. *1961*

Left: Pangnirtung Pass. Mount Asgard, Northwest Territories, with its tabletop peak, reigns majestically over the entrance to Auyuittuq National Park, "the land that never melts." *1984*

Robert W. Service's cabin at Dawson City, Yukon Territory. His poem *The Cremation of Sam McGee* with its reference to the cremation "on the marge of the Lake Lebarge" is part of the legendary lore of the Klondike Gold Rush of 1898. *1961*

A watch chain made of gold nuggets found in the
gravels of the placer gold fields of the Dawson City,
Yukon Territory area. *1961*

A little girl and her dog, taken at Carcross, Yukon
Territory. *1961*

Two Inuit children. They represent the future of Nunavik, Canada's newest territory. Seventy-five per cent of the Inuit in Canada still speak Inuktitut, although English and French are taught in schools. *1982*